Introduction

Ceramic painting is an ancient art form that derived from the desire to beautify the simple tools of hearth and home. It has now reached a state of expression that ranges from museum art to interior design. Imagine creating a gorgeous heirloom platter, from start to finish, right in your own home. With the new thermo-hardening ceramic paints now available, which require only a domestic oven to ensure permanent, dishwasher-safe results, you can do just that!

In this book, I will show you how to create your own beautiful and lasting designs with easy-to-follow, step-by-step instructions. Through simple and more involved techniques, you will be able to explore the many facets of ceramic painting with confidence, even if you have no artistic training. And you can easily wash off any mistakes, so don't be afraid to jump right in! I supply all the templates, stencils, and color suggestions you'll need, along with those wonderful helpful hints that come with experience. Once you've tried the wide array of tools and sure-fire techniques presented here—and experienced your own artistic success—you'll have your own ideas for transforming plain china into colorful creations. So let's start with some basics and then move on to the inspiring projects.

Assembling Your Supplies

Ceramic painting can be done at home with a few basic supplies, some of which you probably already have in your kitchen or bath: blank china pieces, cotton swabs, sponges, and paper towels. The rest are easily found in your local art supply, craft, or hobby stores. I will recommend where to find any special items mentioned in a project, and whenever possible, I will suggest recycled substitutes for items purchased in stores.

Choosing Your Ceramics

You may use any glazed ceramic, china, or porcelain piece you like for this kind of painting. Just keep in mind that if you choose unglazed ceramics, you'll need to treat them with a special sealant (see page 15). In addition to department, import, and craft stores, specialty home and kitchen stores now abound with interesting ceramic wares. Search your own cupboards for old, tired, or even chipped china that a splash of colorful paint could transform. Second-hand shops and yard sales are another rich source of inexpensive and unique pieces.

Ceramic Choices I like the neutral background of white and ivory ceramic, china, or porcelain pieces. But you can think beyond white; yellow is a great base for warm greens and orange-reds, and the lighter opaque colors and the sparkling metallics show up on even the darkest surfaces.

Ceramic Paints Shown here is just a small sampling of the colors available in the line of water-based ceramic paints I use. As you can see, they come in small jars and as markers and outliners, and they are also available in glittering metallics like gold, silver, and pewter. The swatches show the types of strokes each produces.

Selecting Your Paints

A variety of ceramic paints are available,, ranging from water-based to solvent-based and from washable to nonwashable. I use water-based, thermo-hardening ceramic paints, outliners, and markers that are baked in an ordinary kitchen oven. The paints range from glossy and transparent to matte and opalescent. They produce a permanent, dishwasher- and food-safe finish that is smooth and lustrous. The paints are nontoxic and, until baked, clean up easily with water. (Not all ceramic paints are lead-free, so check your labels.) They also mix beautifully, so you can create your own blends. Just be sure to include a diluting agent or thinner along with your paint purchase, as water weakens the paints' thermo-hardening properties.

Ceramic Painting

by Diana Fisher

The author would like to thank Fred Sullenberger
for his technical support and photography.
The author and publisher would like to express their gratitude
to Pébéo, and to Angela Scherz in particular,
for their generous gifts of time and supplies.

Walter Foster Publishing, Inc.
23062 La Cadena Drive
Laguna Hills, CA 92653
www.walterfoster.com

Contents

Introduction 3

Assembling Your Supplies 4

Before You Begin 6

A Treasury of Tiles: A Few Basic Techniques 8

Colorful Flower Garden: Using Sponges and Flat Brushes 14

Nasturtium Vase: Sponging and Freehand Painting 17

Picturesque Pitcher: Decorative Relief Painting 20
    Glass Templates 23

Traditional Sushi and Sake Set: Drawing with Markers 24
    Sushi and Sake Set Templates 27

Country Kitchen Canisters: Stenciling and Basket Weaves 28
    Canister Templates 31

Curious Cat Coffee Cup: Opaque Painting and Removing Color 32
    Coffee Cup Templates 35

Majolica Soup Tureen: History as Inspiration 36
    Soup Tureen Templates 40

Decorative Cloisonné Plate: Two Ways to Use Outliners 41
    Plate Templates 45

Glittering Beaded Boxes: Painting and Embellishing 46
    Box Templates 49

Elegant Holiday Platter: Masking and Marbleizing 50
    Platter Templates 53

Rosy Bath Ensemble: Stylized Imagery 54
    Bath Ensemble Template 57

Regal Rose Teapot: Flat Washes and Painting with Metallics 58
    Teapot Templates 63

A World of Possibilities 64

Using Painting Tools

You can do almost everything with a round brush, but I recommend also getting a wide, flat brush for painting washes and covering large areas. Sponges are great for creating textures, and they can be found in craft stores in both fine and coarse grains. I also use squeeze bottles to spread the paint by letting it run and merge, producing a softly blended, glassy finish. You can buy these bottles at craft stores, or you can recycle plastic hair-coloring bottles or food containers, such as squeezable mustard bottles (just clean and dry them well).

Brushes and Applicators Stamping, sponging, and squeezing paint from bottles will all produce outstanding, professional-looking results with little effort. In each project in this book, I'll give you detailed instructions on the best ways to use a variety of painting tools.

Palettes My favorite palettes are a plate covered with plastic wrap (changing colors is just a matter of replacing the plastic wrap) and a large ceramic palette, which is heavy enough to stay in place and cleans up beautifully.

Picking a Palette

Palettes come in all shapes and sizes and are available in ceramic, metal, or plastic versions. Ceramic is the most durable and easiest to clean if you're using water-based paint. Ceramic tiles make great palettes for mixing small dabs of paint, and small bowls are handy for the large quantities of paint required for washes and for filling squeeze bottles. Recycled food cans, aluminum trays, plastic containers, chipped or broken china plates or bowls, and even plastic lids also make good palettes.

Handy Extras

Use cotton pads and alcohol for degreasing your ceramics. Keep paper towels on hand for drying your brushes and mopping up spills. Cotton swabs and toothpicks are handy for touching up the edges of your painting or for engraving. A utility knife is also useful for cleaning up edges and for cutting stencils. A ruler is useful for some projects, and artist's tape or masking tape is best for blocking off areas and holding the templates in place. Use a soft lead pencil or a china pencil and graphite-backed transfer paper, available at art supply stores, to draw designs on your piece (see page 25).

Additional Tools Along with the tools listed at left, I use photographer's gloves (found in photography and art supply stores) to keep my fingerprints from contaminating the clean pieces. I cut the fingers off my "painting hand," leaving the little finger longer; that's the finger I use to rest my hand as I paint.

Before You Begin

Setting Up Your Work Station

You don't need a formal studio for ceramic painting, but you do want a work surface that's flat and level. A tabletop is ideal. Cover it with white paper, newsprint, or an old tablecloth to protect it from spills. Newspaper end rolls are an inexpensive option that are sometimes available at your local newspaper offices.

Your Work Station Make sure your space is well lit and well ventilated, and don't forget to treat yourself to a nice, comfortable chair!

Cleaning Ceramic Surfaces

It's important to clean and degrease every ceramic surface before painting on it, as dirt and oils can interfere with the paints' ability to adhere. Try a solution of denture cleaner and hot water for tough stains and hard-to-reach areas like bottlenecks. Remove sticky price labels with an adhesive solvent or nail polish remover, but first get off as much of the paper as possible.

Prepping the Surface Before painting, make sure to clean the surface. I use alcohol on a cotton pad—great for degreasing—then wipe away any fibers from the pad with a paper towel.

Washing Away Mistakes

Water-based, thermo-hardening ceramic paints are water-soluble until you bake them. This means that whatever you're not completely satisfied with can be easily removed with plain water! To remove the more stubborn outliner paint, soak your piece, and then scrape off the bulk with a knife. Don't scrape too hard, or you may leave metal marks on your china. Wash off any remaining paint with warm water.

Beginning Again You can remove small areas with a wet cotton swab or rinse away an entire painting session in your kitchen sink. The paint hardens as it dries, so you might need to soak the piece in warm water first to loosen the paint.

Baking Your Creation

Baking requirements vary among the different paint brands; the paints I use in this book call for 24 hours (48 hours for outliners) of air-drying time before being baked. After that, I place the piece in a cold oven and set the temperature at 325°F (160°C). Once the temperature stabilizes, I bake for 30 minutes, and then turn the oven off and let the piece cool completely.

Finalizing Your Efforts The best thing about thermo-hardening ceramic paints is that you can "fire" them at home in an ordinary kitchen oven, making them permanent.

Troubleshooting

Problem: The paint is too streaky.	**Probable Cause:** There isn't enough paint on the brush.	**Solution:** Load more paint on your brush so it flows out and flattens, or add a little thinner to the paint to improve the flow.
Problem: Bubbles form while baking.	**Probable Cause:** The paint didn't air-dry long enough before baking.	**Solution:** Check the label on your paints for the correct drying time; most require at least 24 hours before baking.
Problem: The colors turn brownish when they're baked.	**Probable Cause:** The paint burned.	**Solution:** Use an oven thermometer to check your oven's temperature, and make sure you use the correct setting.
Problem: The paints do not withstand dishwashing well.	**Probable Cause:** The paints have been improperly used or diluted.	**Solution:** Make sure your ceramic surface is properly degreased, that the paints are not diluted with water, and that you followed the baking instructions.
Problem: The paint in the markers does not flow.	**Probable Cause:** The markers have not been prepped.	**Solution:** Be patient; shake vigorously, and then press down on the tip for several seconds to get the paint flowing.

A Treasury of Tiles: A Few Basic Techniques

Painting Methods

Before you begin with a whole project, it's a good idea to acquaint yourself with a few basic ceramic painting techniques. Gaining some familiarity with the paints and getting a little practice with your tools will help you proceed with confidence and creativity. Here I'll demonstrate some methods of painting on ceramic. You don't have to copy exactly what I paint here; experiment with your own designs. You can always wash it all off and save your tiles for another time. Remember: There is no right or wrong. Art is subjective; if you like it, it's good!

Brush Painting Round brushes are my most useful tools, although I also use "specialty" brushes for specific purposes. A great technique for florals is "one-stroke" painting, where each petal and leaf is achieved in one stroke. To start, press down with a round brush; then lift the brush to taper off the stroke as you move toward the center. A round "liner" brush is perfect for making long, thin strokes. A flat brush can be loaded with two colors, one on each side, to produce a variegated color—great for leaf sections. By holding an angled brush upright and stroking along its edge, you can make thin lines. A wide, flat brush is used to cover large areas with a wash, to blend colors, or for making quick, overlapping strokes.

Sponge Painting Sponges create texture easily and evenly, and you can cover large areas quickly. Fine-grained sponges, found at craft stores, produce a delicate texture. Coarse-grained sponges, such as common kitchen sponges, yield a rougher texture. Just dip the sponge in a generous amount of paint, blot the excess off onto your palette, and dab the color on, pinching the sponge a bit to prevent getting hard edges. To achieve a marbled effect, begin by sponging with a coarse sponge in one color and letting it dry. Then sponge over this layer (sparingly) with a darker color, using a ripped and ragged piece of sponge (see page 13 for creating a faux stone look).

Drawing and Pouring on the Color

Ceramic paint markers allow you to draw designs, rather than painting them. The markers work like regular felt-tip markers, but the thinned paint in them dries quickly; if you draw over dried paint, you may disrupt it. With squeeze bottles, you can cover large areas with a multitude of colors. Fill your bottles with diluted paint, hold up your ceramic piece, and squeeze the color on. Use one bottle at a time, and let the colors run, merge, and drip right off the piece. When you're done, set the piece down to allow the colors to settle into place. (It's a good idea to cover your work surface with newsprint to absorb the excess paint, and you may want to wear plastic gloves to protect your hands.)

Taking Paint Away A fast way to engrave is to comb the paint out (see page 11 for more on combing). To engrave with a cotton swab, drag or swirl it through wet paint, changing ends as the tip becomes saturated. A toothpick is another good engraving tool; it works best when the paint has dried a little, but not too much. To etch with a utility knife, start with a wash to cover the area; try to get the wash as thin as possible while retaining maximum color coverage. Darker colors or opaque colors work best and provide good contrast to the etched areas. After the paint has dried thoroughly, sketch in your design with the tip of a utility knife. Then begin to scrape away the paint with your etching tool.

Stenciling and Masking For a simple design, sponge or brush the paint onto a stamp, and press the stamp evenly onto the ceramic surface (for more on stamping, see page 11). I use transparent tape for masking (I found that it produces a cleaner edge than masking tape), but I also use paper frisket or liquid masking (found in art supply and craft stores). To mask, place your masking medium over the areas you want to remain uncolored, and then wash color on top. It is important to remove tape and frisket while the paint is wet, but you must wait until the paint has dried before you remove the liquid mask. You can also use stencils instead of masking. Cut out stencils with a utility knife, and then tape them into place before sponging.

Stamping and Combing

Stamping and combing are both wonderful methods of creating a range of repeating patterns, striped effects, and professional-looking designs. Both methods are also simple to execute and capable of covering large areas quickly. Here I will use those versatile tiles again—this time to demonstrate basic combing, as well as a variety of stamping techniques with different tools. Later in the book, you'll find other projects that highlight or combine these painting techniques. For these demonstrations, you can use commercial rubber combs and stamps, which are available in varying sizes and designs in the faux painting section of most craft stores. But I'll also show you how to make your own so you can unleash your own creativity.

Creating Your Own Treasury Design doesn't get much easier than stamping. And tiles, because they are flat, provide beautiful canvases for stamping and combing. What a great way to accent your kitchen or bath décor!

Basic Combing Begin with a flat wash of color over the tile. Don't make it too thick, or the combed lines will fill in. While the paint is wet, drag the comb through it, keeping even pressure across the comb. If two passes are needed, line up the comb at the edge of the last line and follow it down. For circular sections, rotate the comb. You can also pencil in your design first, and then paint and comb a section at a time. Clean up the edges with a moist cotton swab, and allow the paint to dry in-between sections. To keep the lines straight and square, brace the tile against a phone book, and pull the comb down, using the book spine as a guide. To make your own cardboard comb, measure out the teeth with a ruler, and cut them out with a utility knife.

Basic Stamping I've found that the best way to get ceramic paint on a stamp is to use a stencil brush. Dab on the paint evenly, and press the stamp to the tile surface steadily; then carefully lift, taking care that the stamp does not slide. To create an alternating pattern, stamp one color at a time, thoroughly washing the stamp between colors. You can also turn leaves into pretty stamps; just remember to dab the paint on the underside, where the vein pattern is raised, so that your stamped image has some character. I found some lace border in a craft store and thought I'd try stamping with it. It worked beautifully! Make sure to press down evenly over the entire section of lace so that the pattern shows up completely.

Potato Stamping Make your own stamp by carving a potato! Cut a potato in half (or fourths, as your design warrants). Use a good kitchen paring knife or your utility knife to draw a design into it; then cut away around it until your design is left in relief (raised). Try using cookie cutters for larger designs. Next dry the potato carefully with a paper towel, and dab on the paint with the stencil brush. Take care not to load it too heavily with paint. Then press the stamp down on your tile. The result is a rustic and charming design that is yours alone.

11

Foam Stamping Commercially made foam stamps are readily available, but you can easily make your own from sheets of foam purchased from craft or hobby stores. Cut your design from a piece of thin foam with either scissors or a utility knife. Glue this piece to a rectangle of thick foam, which will serve as the handle. When the glue has dried, apply the paint to the raised foam design, and press the stamp down on your tile. Now you'll have the satisfaction of knowing that your design is both hand-made and original!

Stamping as an Outline Many commercially made stamps are designed to be accented with painted-in color. Most of these designs are very intricate and too detailed to work with ceramic paints, which are thicker than stamping inks. Choose a simple design, and keep a steady hand when you stamp, so the lines stay clear. You can always follow the image on the front of the stamp as a guide for coloring. For a different twist, try stamping with metallic gold or another color instead of black—then use a small round brush to fill in the design with color.

Combing with Masking To make this combed border design, measure 3/4" from the edge and draw a straight line. Then use a circle template (such as a coin) to mark half-circles along the line with your china pencil. Apply low-tack, easy-peel frisket to the tile, and cut along the scalloped line using a utility knife with a fresh blade. Peel up the ends of the frisket, leaving the middle intact, and press the edges firmly. Paint on color with a flat brush, stroking away from the frisket. Comb through the color, and then carefully remove the frisket while the paint is still wet. Dip a cotton swab in paint to stamp the polka dots and flowers, checking frequently to make sure that the tip does not become too saturated and that the fibers don't come loose.

Creating a Faux Stone Look

Faux painting is a popular style of decorative painting, and it can be seen on everything from fireplace mantels to cardboard boxes—and now ceramic tiles! Here I will demonstrate faux stone painting using a sponge, a commercially produced rubber stamp, a strand of chenille (pipe cleaner), and a stencil brush. Choose a stamp that coordinates with your kitchen décor, and you'll have a beautiful finished piece to display on a wall or countertop.

Step One Measure 1-1/4" (or however wide you want your border) from the edges, and mark all four sides with your china pencil. Using your ruler as a straightedge, draw the lines all the way across each side so that they overlap at the corners. Painting with a sponge can be very messy, so you might want to wear protective gloves for this project (see page 5).

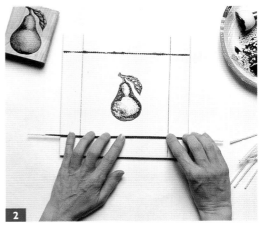

Step Two Choose a stamp with an image that can be filled in with color, and stamp it in the center of the tile. Then use a stencil brush to generously apply paint to a strand of chenille. Line it up with your pencil marks, and press down, keeping the chenille relatively straight. You need to press hard enough to get good coverage, but not so hard that the paint spreads and blobs up.

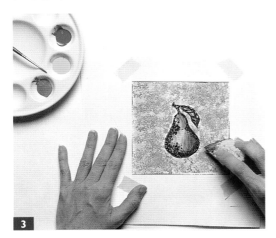

Step Three Make sure your center image is completely dry before you fill it in with color. Then use paper to block off the areas to be faux painted, one section at a time. Sponge your first layer in a light color with a coarse, flat sponge. Wait a few minutes for that to dry, and then sponge on your second, darker layer with a rough, torn piece of sponge. For the background, cover the center image with cut paper, or use a cotton swab to paint around the edges.

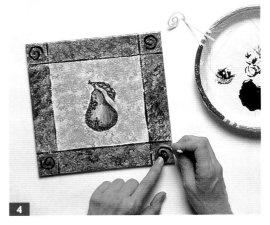

Step Four Now finish your design with spirals, squiggles, or whatever else you can dream up. You can paint on details with a brush or create your final touches by bending chenille strips into shapes and dipping them in paint. (You may want to practice on paper first to see what kind of coverage you'll get.) Are you happy with the result? Then bake your creation to make the paint permanent, and enjoy your faux masterpiece!

Colorful Flower Garden: Using Sponges and Flat Brushes

Simple patterns and bright color schemes perfectly complement an outdoor or indoor garden of plants and flowers. Explore the different pot shapes and watering cans available at nurseries, home improvement stores, and craft stores, and pick some that coordinate with your house and garden style. Then you can cleverly stamp a plain or painted metal watering can to match your painted pots. Just make sure your pots have a protective glaze; otherwise, you'll need to seal them yourself before painting (see the box on page 15).

Fantastic Flower Pots These delightful pots are great projects for beginners: The techniques are simple, and the effects are beautiful. They also make wonderful gifts—if you can part with them!

Step One First decide the shapes for your design; I chose a circle and a square. With a marker, draw the shapes on a fine-grained sponge, and then cut them out with scissors. Don't worry if your shapes aren't perfect. Irregular edges will add a homemade charm to the finished product. Next work out your color scheme (see the box on page 16). For this project, I chose emerald and ruby tones in subdued shades and a purple that I discovered was a little too bright. Rather than toning down the purple with black (which would darken it) or white (which would lighten it), I muted it with yellow—its complementary color.

Step Two After degreasing your pot, draw a rough guide-line around the midpoint of the upper portion of the lip with a china pencil. Then dip your square sponge in paint, and press it to the pot, rocking the sponge around gently to cover the curved surface. As you move around the pot, be careful not to touch the paint you have already sponged, and do not rest the top of the pot on your work surface. If you are copying my design, you may want to gauge the positioning of your squares by testing it out beforehand, so you'll know how much overlap you'll need to make the design come out even at the end.

Sealing Ceramics

Unglazed terra cotta pots can also be decorated with ceramic paints and baked, as long as they are sealed first. (Otherwise the paints will be absorbed into the clay, and the colors will look muddy.) Many craft and ceramic shops carry a wide selection of bisque items that they can glaze for you, or you can seal them yourself at home. For maximum coverage and gloss, use a sealant that's made for porous surfaces, and follow the directions on the label.

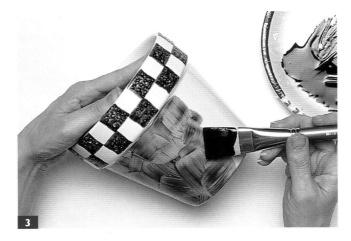

Step Three For the base, use the same color you used to sponge on the top motif. When painted instead of sponged on, it will appear lighter than the top and will provide a pleasing contrast. With a wide, flat brush, cover the base of the pot with short, quick, overlapping strokes, turning the brush as you go so that the final effect is a sort of random weave of angled brushstrokes.

Step Four For the watering can, start by sponging on shapes dipped in white. This will provide a background for colors that otherwise might not show up well on a dark background. After the white areas dry, you can sponge whatever colors you like on top. I left some white as part of the design on this watering can, to match my pots. And don't worry; plain or prepainted metal can be baked in the oven along with your ceramic pieces. Be sure to let them air-dry the recommended length of time before baking them. Once they're baked, they'll be ready to adorn your garden!

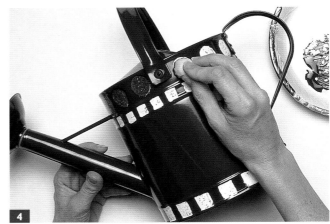

Choosing a Color Scheme

When working out a color scheme, play with the colors on paper first, before putting paint to your ceramic. A color wheel is a great form of reference for developing a scheme. The color wheel shown here is made up of the three primary colors (red, blue, and yellow) and the three secondary colors (purple, green, and orange). Colors opposite each other on the wheel are called *complementary* colors; they exhibit the greatest amount of contrast when placed next to each other. When you want a muted or more subdued tone of a color, mix it with a little of its complement.

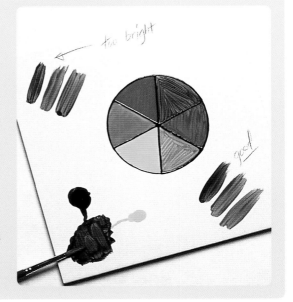

Nasturtium Vase: Sponging and Freehand Painting

Sponging is an easy way to cover a large area with even color and to create pleasing textures in varying degrees. Experiment with the different effects you can achieve by using different types of sponges and mixing the colors as you sponge. Try sponging colors on together while they're still wet, or layer them and let the colors dry between layers.

Floral Vase These elegant nasturtiums, scattered over a textured background and framed in a cloud of pink, are ideal decorations for this vase. The technique for painting the flower petals and leaves is dramatic and very effective against the sponged surface.

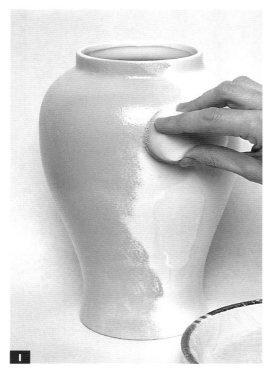

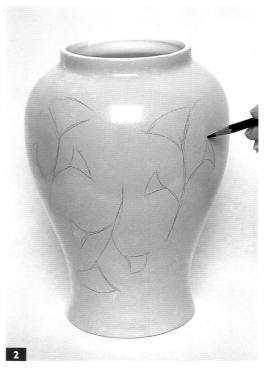

Step One After degreasing the vase, select a background color, or custom-mix your own. By mixing amber with white, I created a light beige. Using a fine-grained sponge, dab paint onto your vase (pinch the sponge a bit to keep the edges soft). To even out the color and texture of your background, sponge over it a second time using less paint.

Step Two When the sponged paint is completely dry to the touch, roughly sketch in the nasturtiums with a china pencil. For each flower, draw a long, curving stem, side stems, and triangles as rough placements for the blossoms. Sketch as you go around the vase, arbitrarily placing flowers in various positions to fit the space available.

Step Three Select three colors for the nasturtiums: a light value for the main color, a medium value for contrast, and a darker value for shadowing. Now triple-dip a large round brush: First dip it all the way into the lightest color; next dip the loaded brush halfway into the medium color, and finally dip the tip into the darkest color. (You might want to practice creating the flowers on a tile or a piece of paper before painting them on the vase.)

Step Four Place the loaded brush where the top of your petal will begin. Push the brush forward slightly to splay the bristles open, and then pull the brush back gently, lifting as you go toward the stem. Create three petals in this manner, side by side, with the center petal slightly higher. (Clean your brush between petals.) Then dip your brush into the two darkest colors, and paint two more petals in front of the others while the paint is still wet.

Step Five Paint the stems in with an angled brush. You can use a round brush if that's all you have, but an angled brush works particularly well for long lines on a curved surface. Paint all the stems on all the flowers, turning the vase carefully. Be sure not to touch or set the vase down on the flowers you've already painted.

Step Six Select a color for the leaves that's lighter than the stems. If you combine this color with both your stem color and the shadow color from your flower petals, you'll have light, medium, and dark values once again. Using the same technique as you did for the petals, paint the middle of the leaf with a single stroke. Then paint the left and right sides of the leaf the same way, overlapping a bit in the center.

Step Seven Next pick another color for the background. I mixed my flower color with amber and then added white to soften the color, because I didn't want the background to compete with my main design. Load the sponge sparingly with color, dabbing it on your palette first to remove excess paint. Pinch the sponge, and dab color on gently between the flowers, creating a cloudlike effect. Let the paint air-dry the recommended length of time, and then bake your vase. Now you're ready to fill this gorgeous vase with beautiful flowers and show off your work!

Picturesque Pitcher: Decorative Relief Painting

Relief motifs on ceramic offer the opportunity to combine lustrous color with a sculptured, three-dimensional look. This is also an ideal project for beginners because the design is already in place and the softly delineated boundaries are very forgiving. Most art and craft or hobby stores—plus home, import, and department stores—carry pitchers, plates, and figurines that can be transformed into your own works of art!

Relief Pitcher Ceramic paint brings this white-on-white relief pitcher to life with dazzling color. It's easy to create a stunning place setting by painting glasses to match, which can be baked in the oven at the same time.

Step One This is a good time to wear cotton gloves to keep the degreased surface clean as you paint. After experimenting with different ways to paint the relief on this pitcher, I settled on leaving some white space in my design; it became too confusing when I butted the colors against each other. Experiment with your piece before you begin (remember that water easily removes the paint before it's baked). Then start with the grapes, and cover each with bright purple. After the paint has dried a bit, paint a shadow on the underside of each grape in one stroke with a darker purple. You will be moving around the whole piece, so take care not to touch or set your piece down on any area you have painted.

Step Two Paint each leaf completely with a bright green. Let them dry, and then define each leaf with a darker green using short, separate strokes that follow the serrated edge of the leaf. Add dark green veins with either a thin round brush, an angled brush, or a liner.

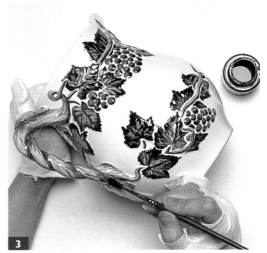

Step Three Paint the vines, stems, and handle with yellow ochre. When they're dry, paint a shadow beneath the stems and vines with red ochre. On the handle, use a drybrush technique: Wipe excess paint off your brush on paper to "dry" it, and then lightly stroke in the shadows.

21

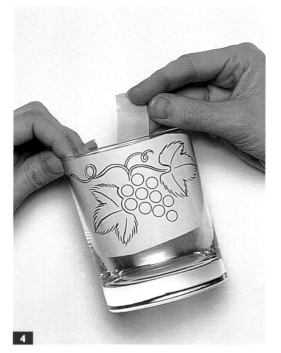

4

5

Step Four I provide grape templates on page 23, but you can draw your own template design to match your pitcher. Draw or photocopy the template to the appropriate size, cut it out, and tape it in place to the inside of the glass. Remove it carefully when you are done so you can reuse it for all the glasses you paint.

Step Five For the glasses, use all the same colors you used for the pitcher. Since the glass is clear, the resulting design will be softer, which complements the brilliant ceramic imagery. Paint the background colors first; then remove the template (to see better) and add the shadows. Now bake your pieces and set a beautiful table!

Shades of Creativity

Not only can you paint on glass with ceramic paints, but you can paint on plastic as well. Plastic cannot be baked, however, so let the paint set a few days before use, and wipe it with a soft, dry cloth to clean it. Transform a pair of plain reading glasses from boring to beautiful with a series of confetti-like colors. Painting white zebra stripes on this black pair of sunglasses makes a unique and fashionable accessory.

Glass Templates

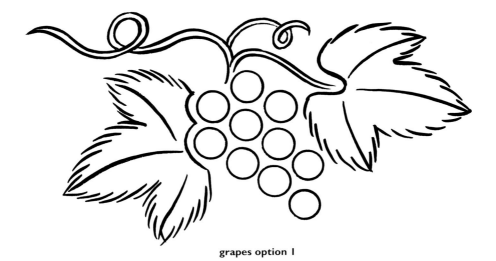

grapes option 1

grapes option 2

Photocopy each template, enlarging or reducing it as needed to fit your glasses. See page 25 for transfer instructions.

Traditional Sushi and Sake Set: Drawing with Markers

Instead of painting, you can also draw your designs with ceramic paint markers. Markers are easier to control than brushes are because the tips are stable and produce an even flow of paint. The markers are perfect for drawing detailed pictures such as the pagoda scene below. Children will also love to create fun projects with ceramic paint markers. The ceramic paints are nontoxic and wash off easily with water. However, I recommend that children be supervised, especially during the baking process. Be sure to explain that while they're creating their design, they should try not to touch what they have already drawn.

Intricate Details Using ceramic paint markers to create these traditional Asian designs made drawing the details a cinch. While I have chosen this monochromatic blue look, a variety of bright colors could be equally stunning.

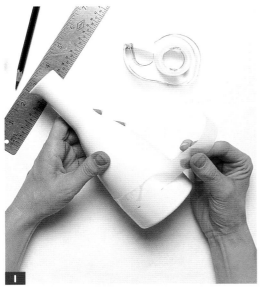

Step One Measure 1" from the bottom of a degreased sake bottle and 1-1/2" from the edge of the sushi tray—these measurements may vary according to your pieces and your preference—and make marks with a china pencil. Place a strip of transparent tape along the marks, above the area to be combed. In Step Two, you'll need to work quickly so the paint doesn't have a chance to dry.

Step Two With a flat brush, wash your color on evenly, but don't make it too thick. Keeping even pressure on the comb, pull the comb downward to the edge. For the next pass, align a tooth of the comb with the last line combed, and follow that line as you pull. Immediately remove the tape. Clean up any extra paint with a moist cotton swab, and let the paint dry completely before continuing.

Step Three Copy the bottle template, and tape it over transfer paper. If you don't have transfer paper, use the side of a pencil to cover the back of the template with graphite. Starting with the horizon, line up the transfer paper and template with the edge of the combed blue, cutting the paper as needed to conform to the curve. Trace over the lines with a ballpoint pen, and carefully remove the paper.

Step Four Get the blue marker flowing by shaking vigorously and pressing on the tip for several seconds. Draw the details, following the template as a guide. Use small circles to represent the tree foliage and straight lines for the roofing. Draw in short strokes toward the bush line to create a shadow. Fill in with random lines on the ground to add interest. Take care not to damage the combed paint.

5

6

Step Five Allow the marker drawing to dry, or bake your piece before proceeding. Then choose a blue from your jar paints that's close to the marker blue, and mix up two variations with thinner, making one more diluted than the other. Using a soft brush, lightly paint in the color, varying the two values to add depth.

Step Seven After the paint has dried, go over your drawing again with the blue marker. Emphasize some lines—use the template as a guide—and darken any lines that seem too light. Be careful not to work the marker too much over the existing color, or you may break up the paint. When you're finished with the sake bottle, follow the same method for the cups and tray. Then bake and enjoy! Sushi, anyone?

Step Six Add the clouds in the sky and the water ripples with your lightest diluted blue. The clouds can be any shape, but I suggest keeping all the ripples parallel to the horizon line. You can use the template provided, or you can paint the ripples freehand, but stagger them to make them look more realistic.

7

Rendering with Markers

Ceramic paint markers come in many colors and produce wonderful results. The effects can be brilliant! The marker paints dry quickly, so blending and layering are sometimes difficult, but don't let this deter you from experimenting! Use them as you would any markers or crayons by coloring in your design section by section, butting the colors up against each other but not overlapping. If you'd rather, leave some white space between each color for a more stylized look.

Sushi and Sake Set Templates

sake bottle

tray

water ripples

sake cups

Photocopy each template, enlarging or reducing as needed to fit your ceramic pieces. See page 25 for transfer instructions.

Country Kitchen Canisters:
Stenciling and Basket Weaves

Brighten up your kitchen with stenciled roosters and a beautiful basket-weave pattern in gorgeous colors. I chose autumn colors for our barnyard friends, but feel free to create a palette that matches your décor or strikes your fancy. You might also vary the project by painting each rooster in a different color, rather than the subtle changes I have made in variation. Or draw your own stylized versions. The choice is yours; be creative!

Canister Set Brighten your kitchen with these rooster and basket-weave canisters in gorgeous autumn colors. The stencil-and-sponge technique is quick and easy, and it produces a wonderfully textured finish.

Step One Transfer the basket-weave templates onto the top of the lid and the lower portion of the cleaned canister. Use fewer rows of the weave pattern on your smallest canister and more on the largest. Center the lid template visually, and leave some space between the canister template and the bottom of the canister. This will leave a clean, white edge after you've painted the basket-weave border.

Step Two Mask off the edge of the lid by notching the masking tape so that it will lie flat around the rim. Mask off the center square with transparent tape, covering the square entirely. (I used clear tape here so I could see where the edges were.) This is where you'll paint your label. Try not to tape over the transferred weave design; the design may come up with the tape when you peel it off.

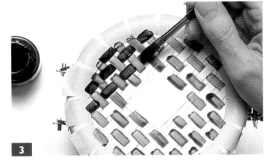

Step Three With light green and a 1/4" flat brush, make a single stroke in each horizontal bar of the weave, always moving toward your painting hand. Let the paint dry until tacky. Then paint the perpendicular bars in a similar manner with darker green, as shown. When the paint has dried, pierce it with a utility knife along the edge of the masking. Pull off all the tape. Then clean up any edges with the knife or a moist cotton swab. Repeat for the canister.

Step Four Copy another lid template, and make a stencil by cutting out the inner square for the label. Line up the cut-out hole directly over the transferred square on the lid, and tape the stencil down on the outer edges. You don't need to tape the entire perimeter—just two spots to hold it in place will do. Sponge yellow ochre over the center square, dabbing gently with a fine-grained sponge until you get an even layer. Carefully lift off the stencil.

Step Five When the sponged paint has dried, paint a black border around the yellow-ochre square label. Then write in the name of the intended contents of the canister in burgundy with a small round brush or a liner. I used my own handwriting, but you may find a typestyle you like that you can print out on your computer and transfer into place on the label.

29

Step Six Cut the square around the rooster template, and then cut out the rooster pieces to make a stencil. Spray the back of the stencil lightly with spray mount, let it dry, and press the stencil into place. Mask the comb, wattle, and legs by taping the cut-out template pieces in place. Sponge on the body colors in varying shades with a fine-grained sponge, and apply black with a torn sponge for a speckled look. When the paint is dry, remove the leg and beak masks, and tape the cut-out body template over the painted body. Sponge yellow over the exposed beak and legs. When dry, mask the beak, and sponge the comb and wattle with red.

Step Seven Carefully remove the beak mask, the body mask, and the outer stencil. Add details to the beak and legs by painting in yellow ochre shadows with a round brush. Add outlines and shadows on the comb and the wattle with burgundy. Create the shadows by painting a thin line along one side and a thicker stroke along the opposite side. Paint in feathers on the rooster's body with a dark color, such as the dark teal shown here. Use short strokes on the body for the small body feathers, and long, sweeping strokes for the large tail feathers.

Step Eight Paint in tufts of grass around the canister just above the basket-weave border. Start with a few strokes of yellow ochre in each tuft, and let this color dry. Then add a few more strokes of light green to each tuft, overlapping the grass blades for added contrast.

Step Nine Dip the end of a cotton swab in burgundy, and stamp it around the grass to represent flowers. Change cotton swabs when the fibers start to come loose, and be careful not to saturate the swab excessively with paint. Air-dry and bake, and enjoy your canister set!

Canister Templates

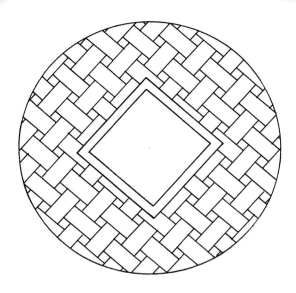

lid basket weave

rooster

**canister
basket weave**

Photocopy each template, enlarging or reducing as needed to fit your canisters. See page 25 for transfer instructions.

Curious Cat Coffee Cup: Opaque Painting and Removing Color

Water-based ceramic paints are generally transparent. But here I will show you how to get even, opaque coverage with just about any color. For this whimsical design, I searched everywhere for just the right cup shape and ended up buying a glazed bisque piece from a ceramic shop. You'll find a great source of ceramic creations and ideas in these stores. Have the bisque glazed for you before you purchase it, or check your line of paints for a food-safe sealing medium, and seal the pieces yourself.

Colorful Cats Opaque ceramic painting is a simple technique, yet the smooth finish it creates makes this fanciful design come alive. It's a wonderful technique for adorning any place setting.

32

Step One Transfer the template designs onto the saucer and cup. If your saucer has an indentation where the cup fits, copy the saucer template to fit. Otherwise, center the template visually. Cut the cup template so that the paper conforms to the convex surface, and place it on your cup so that the cat's tail begins at the top of the cup handle.

Step Two Sketch in the rest of your design with a china pencil. Using the shape of your cup as a guide, make color breaks where there is a natural change in shape. Sketch a borderline around the edge of the saucer. Then draw a line to halve the saucer between the border and the center, and further divide each half into three sections.

Step Three Choose a color for the background behind the cat, and mix it well with white. White is what makes your colors more opaque. Here I mixed emerald green with enough white to create a light aqua. Generously load a large round brush with paint, and stroke very lightly, using the side of the brush (not the tip) to spread and even out the paint. (If the paint is too thick, it will form drips.) If you still want more coverage, let the paint dry and give it a second coat.

Step Four As soon as you have completed the background, make polka dots by removing paint with a cotton swab. Moisten the cotton swab with water, hold it upright, and swirl it in the wet paint. Change cotton swabs with each dot. If you find that your paint has dried so much that it's difficult to get the paint to swirl off, try dipping the cotton swab in a little rubbing alcohol first. Then switch to the clean end of the swab for a second pass with water.

Step Five Wait for the background to dry; this may take a little longer than usual, as the paint will be thick. You can speed up the process with a hair dryer, but make sure to hold it at least 6" from the paint. Mix white with a contrasting color from the background, and fill in the polka dots with color. I mixed a salmon color by combining orange, fuchsia, and white.

Step Six Create a palette with the rest of the colors you intend to use, mixing each with some white. You may want to work out your color scheme beforehand on a tile or a piece of paper to see if the colors are pleasing together (see the box on page 16). Paint the colors into the rest of the design, but don't paint the black parts, the rim of the saucer, or the top and bottom rims of the cup yet.

Step Seven When everything else is dry to the touch, paint the black areas. If you have been holding the cup by the handle, clean it now before you paint. Begin by outlining the cat on both the cup and saucer. Work from the middle out, and take care not to touch your painted surface. Then paint in some black stripes on the handle to represent the cat's tail.

Step Eight If you have been handling the rims of the cup and saucer, clean them before painting them with your mixed colors. If the paints have dried out too much, make fresh mixes. As you match the colors, bear in mind that ceramic paints will darken slightly as they dry.

Step Nine Add black dots to the aqua borders and white dots to the black sections. Now paint a small heart on the inside of the cup to match the heart in the cat, and outline it with black. Bake the pieces, and your colorful set is ready for use!

Coffee Cup Templates

saucer

cup

Photocopy each template, enlarging or reducing as needed to fit your cup and saucer. See page 25 for transfer instructions.

Majolica Soup Tureen: History as Inspiration

Inspiration for ceramic painting can come from endless sources: photographs, fabric, wallpaper, magazines, wrapping paper, paintings, or even nature. I found a rich inspirational source in researching the history of ceramic painting. Majolica is Italian earthenware with an opaque white glaze containing tin oxide. This tin-glaze technique originated in ninth-century Mesopotamia, but it reached its peak of popularity in Italy during the Renaissance and is still in use today. For this project, I'll make some color suggestions, but you can develop your own palette; in this case, the more colorful, the better!

Italian Inspiration Inspired by this colorful Italian theme? You could continue this idea and create more pieces for this set—like a large salad bowl with the word *insalata* on the side or a bread platter with the word *pane* in the center.

Step One Make cuts in the label template so that it will conform to a convex surface. Center it vertically on one or both sides of the cleaned tureen, and tape it down. I centered it visually (a useful hint is to squint your eyes as you center), but you can measure with a ruler to be accurate. Then transfer the design (see page 25).

Step Two With a china pencil, draw scallop shapes along the top rim and the bottom of the tureen. Measure down from the rim, and draw a line around the circumference to indicate where the ribbing will end (mine ends at the bottom of the handle). Then draw vertical ribs as shown.

Tip for Tape

When transferring a design, especially when there are several templates to tape down, it's handy to cut small pieces of masking tape beforehand. I attach them to the edge of the table, along a ruler, or onto any surface close by where I can easily reach them as needed. This way I don't have to stop each time to dispense the tape while I'm trying to hold the template in place.

Step Three Outline the entire design in black, using a liner or a round brush. Ceramic paints are rather thick, so moving the brush along at a slower pace will enable more paint to issue from the bristles; a fast stroke will yield thinner, lighter lines. Try making short "petal" strokes (see one-stroke painting, page 8) to produce a decorative chain effect. With the same technique, paint the ribbed design around the lid handle as well. It's a good idea to bake your piece at this point before adding color, but if you choose not to bake, let the paint dry thoroughly before going on to the next step.

Step Four Prop up the tureen on something stable so you can easily see and reach the areas you want to paint. Pick a strong primary yellow, and paint a wide stroke on the inside of the label. Then fill in the scallops. Use the side handles to turn the tureen as you paint, since you can paint them last. Otherwise, try not to touch the surface, as you may leave fingerprints that will affect the paints' adherence.

Step Five Once the yellow is dry, choose a bright orange to paint a thin stroke in the center of the label. Paint over the yellow and close to the black outline, so that some of the yellow shows. Then paint orange shadows inside the yellow scallops. When the orange is dry, paint three-petaled, scarlet florets in the scallops. Paint the middle petal first and then the others, using the one-stroke method (page 8).

Step Six After the red has dried, paint the label border with a bright green. Then fill in the ribbing on the tureen and the lid with bright peacock blue. Paint each rib one at a time with strokes parallel to the outlines. Steady your hand by resting your little finger on the inside of the rim or below the ribs, where prints can be cleaned off before you paint.

Step Seven Let the blue on the ribbing dry thoroughly. Then paint a shadow beneath the rim scallops and beside each black rib with ultramarine blue. Leave at least half of the peacock blue in each rib showing. Don't worry about getting perfect coverage; visible brushstrokes add to the charm of this hand-painted look.

Step Eight Make several copies of the arabesque templates. Cut them out, and position them around the body of the tureen and the lid. You may want to cut out a floret or two to make the pieces fit together in a balanced manner, especially on the lid. You can use the same piece of transfer paper over and over, but be careful when slipping it out from under the template so you don't smear the lines.

Step Nine Using the same green you used on the label, paint the vines around the entire tureen and the top of the lid. Then color each of the florets with peacock blue, and add scarlet red dots. Remember to keep your hand off the surface you're painting to prevent leaving fingerprints on the ceramic or smearing the transfer lines. Rest your little finger on the bottom of the tureen.

Step Ten If you have been using the side handles to move and turn the tureen and the top handle to turn the lid, clean these off now before you paint them. I used the yellow, orange, and red, respectively, waiting between colors for the paint to dry. Repeat these colors on the lid handle as well.

Step Eleven Paint the end of the ladle to match the tureen. There isn't much room to work with, but ideally you will want to use all of the colors you used on the tureen. I repeated the ribbing and scallops and added one floret. Now just air-dry and bake, and you're ready for *zuppa!*

Soup Tureen Templates

label

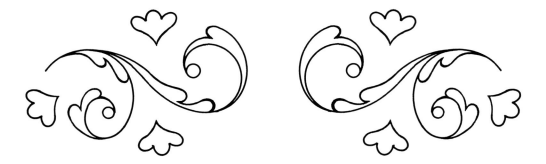

arabesques

Photocopy each template, enlarging or reducing as needed to fit your tureen. See page 25 for transfer instructions.

Decorative Cloisonné Plate:
Two Ways to Use Outliners

This stunning, intricately painted plate will grace any home. It's a piece to be truly proud of artistically, and it is easier to create than you might think. Clever use of the outliners simulates an authentic cloisonné look, while subtle washes suggest fine porcelain painting. The outside panel colors reflect the center motif, bringing the whole design into perfect balance. You can create your own image for the center; perhaps you could render a ship on the sea or a carousel horse—whatever piques your artistic interest.

Metallic Design *Cloisonné* is a term used to describe enamel-painted pieces in which the colored areas are separated by thin metal bands. In this piece, the "metal" is actually metallic ceramic paint squeezed from a tube.

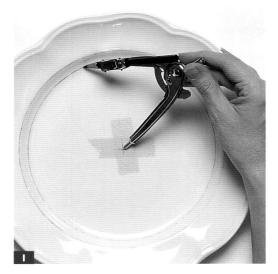

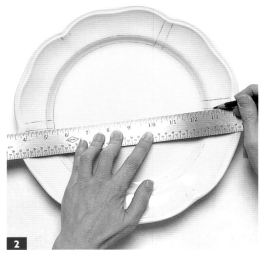

Step One I chose an ivory plate with a decorative rim to better complement the gold outliner. Start by placing an X of tape in the middle of the plate. Then measure the diameter of the plate from its widest points, both left to right and top to bottom. Mark the midpoints. Where these two marks meet will be the center of the plate. Set a compass with a china pencil on this point, and draw a circle at the base of the plate indentation. Open up the compass about 3/8", and draw a circle at the top of the indentation.

Step Two My design has six evenly spaced "notches" along the rim. Pick a distance between the circles—in this case, 3/8"—and draw two lines across the plate border at the six notched points. Here I used a set of compass points to measure off each set of lines, but a ruler or piece of paper that's marked to show the distance will do. Transfer the three border template designs to the six panels in the border. Use two of each, placing like patterns across from each other. Remove the tape from the center of the plate.

Step Three Outline the inner circle with gold; then move outward toward the edge, frequently wiping off the tip of the outliner. Gently drag the outliner along the design, using even pressure. Try making break points where the lines intersect. If you make a mistake, lift the paint off with a moist cotton swab. Air-dry; then bake the plate to set the outliner.

Step Four Transfer the berry template design to the middle of the plate. Remember: The border is geometric and will be displayed with a panel or the border between two panels at its apex. With this in mind, turn the template until you settle on a pleasing position for the interior design. This will be especially important if your design has a definite top.

42

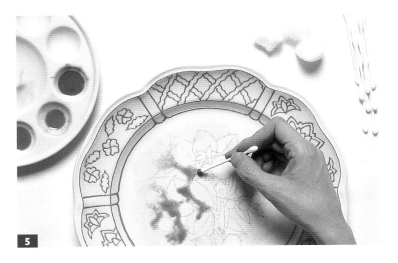

Step Five Dilute a blue and a mauve to thin washes, adding more thinner than paint to make the colors very light and transparent. Using cotton balls, swirl color around the outside of the design, alternating between blue and mauve. Work quickly, so the paint stays wet while you work. Then dilute a slate blue (use less thinner, so the blue is darker), and dab on the color between the berries and leaves with a cotton swab. As you move toward the edge, do not reload the swab with paint; you'll want the color to fade as you go.

Step Six Fill the blackberries in with an amethyst color. Next paint the strawberries, first with a stroke of red on each side and then with a stroke of orange in the middle. For the cherries and blueberries, paint the darker color around the perimeter first, and then swirl a lighter color in the middle. Paint the leaves one half at a time. Make a stripe of light green, and fill in the rest with dark green, stroking in the direction of veins. Make the blackberry leaves by pulling burgundy through the mauve and green, and use red ochre for the stems.

Step Seven When the paint has dried, outline the berries, leaves, and stems with gold outliner. Clean the outliner tip frequently as you paint. Also, hold the plate up as you work, so you can reach the areas to paint without touching the wet colors or the border. Don't forget to add seeds to the strawberries! Use short, thin lines and stagger them. Create the blackberries with a series of tiny circles, beginning at the center and adding more circles as you move toward the edge.

43

Step Eight Choose a background color, and generously load your brush with paint. Hold the plate up to keep the paint as level as possible to prevent pooling. Aiming for even, solid coverage, fill in the section between the outlines, taking care to paint up to the outline. If your paint spills over, lift the paint off with a clean, moistened brush. Then dry the brush, and pick up any excess water. When you finish a section, let it dry flat or use a hair dryer (holding it at least 6" from the paint) to dry it to the tacky stage.

Step Nine Painting one panel at a time, hold the plate as level as possible to keep the paint from pooling. Work at a good pace while painting the background, since you have a lot of area to cover. But be careful; you don't want to paint over your outlined design. If you have to paint next to a spot where the paint has dried, try to butt up against it rather than working your brush over it. Aim for a level (not lumpy) seam. Here I repeated the berry colors in the panels and used the blueberry colors for the weave.

The Artist's Signature

Be proud of your artistic accomplishments in ceramic painting—sign your work! Make a record of the date or year for posterity. Your piece may be handed down as a family heirloom or given as a treasured gift, and its value will increase with the artist's signature. You can sign the back or the bottom of a piece, depending on the design. I usually sign my plates on the back, where there is plenty of space.

Step Ten When the panels are dry, the final step is to add dots to your design with the gold outliner. Remember to clean the outliner tip frequently, and try to maintain even pressure on the outliner tube to produce uniformly sized dots. Bake and proudly display your gorgeous artwork!

44

Plate Templates

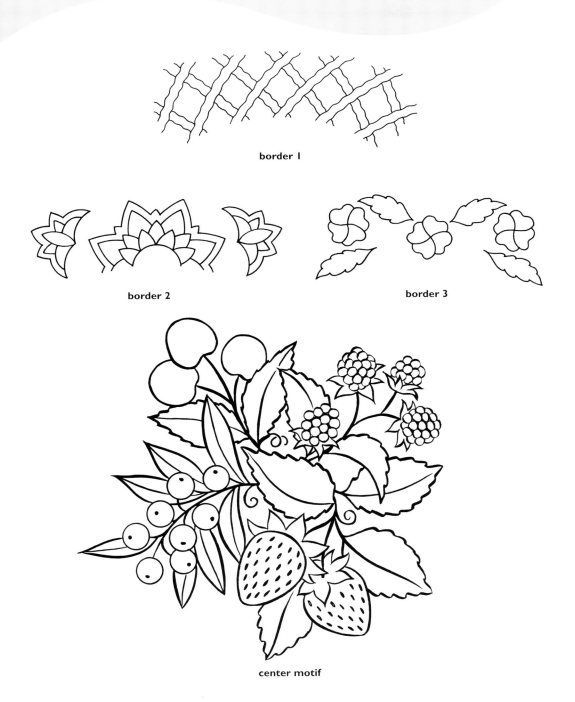

border 1

border 2

border 3

center motif

Photocopy each template, enlarging or reducing as needed to fit your plate. See page 25 for transfer instructions.

Glittering Beaded Boxes: Painting and Embellishing

If you have never visited a bead shop, you're in for a dazzling experience! An endless array of gorgeously colored glass and crystal beads are available in multiple shapes, sizes, and designs. You can also find a selection of beads in art and craft stores; just make sure to get glass or crystal (not plastic), since the beads will be baked. Squeeze-bottle painting is an ideal accompaniment to embellishment with beads, and it is a quick and easy way to get a shimmering, glasslike coverage.

Beautiful Beaded Boxes Beads and jewels add dimension and sparkle to your piece, while squeeze-bottle painting adds color and shimmer. Ceramic boxes are perfect for these techniques, and they make lovely gifts.

Step One For a round box, reduce or enlarge the round template as needed, and transfer the design onto the lid of the box. Adjust the center shape to fit the size and shape of the jewel you'll be using. Or you might opt to fill the center area with beads as an alternative to using a jewel.

Step Two Outline the design, starting in the middle and working outward, but do not outline the circle for the jewel. Keep even pressure on the outliner tube, and try to make stops at the joints of the design to ensure a smooth line. To fit my color scheme, I chose red and blue outliners.

Step Three Paint the bottom of the jewel with color, and set this aside to dry upside down. After the outliner has dried at least to the tacky stage, paint each section of the beaded portion of the design, one at a time. Generously paint in a color that's close to the color of the beads you'll be using. Sprinkle the beads onto the wet paint, and then immediately arrange them with a toothpick so they fill the section neatly. Place larger beads individually with tweezers, and remove stray beads with the clean end of a toothpick.

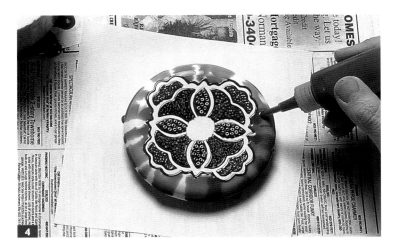

Step Four Clean off the perimeter of the lid, and set the pieces up off your work surface. Dilute the paints to about 7 parts paint to 1 part thinner, and pour them into the squeeze bottles. Quickly squirt on the first color, starting at the edge of the outliner. Guide the color down with the tip of the bottle, and let the paint run off the bottom. Don't cover the area completely. Apply the next color while the first is still wet. When you are done, run a swab under each piece to prevent drips from accumulating.

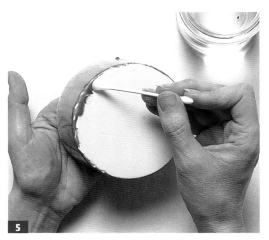

Step Five When paint has dried, clean the bottoms of your pieces with moist cotton swabs. Even though the bottom of your project won't show, this quick cleanup will give your box a finished, professional look..

Step Six Paint some clear ceramic paint medium (which will now act as a glue) onto the bottom of the jewel, over the dried paint. Place the jewel in the center of the lid, and press it firmly in place.

Step Seven Boxes are ideal for conveying hidden messages! Paint the bottom of the inside of the box generously with color so that it evens out into a smooth finish. Once it's dry, paint your special message with a brush, or write it with a ceramic paint marker. Finally, let the box air-dry, and then bake it. Now you'll have a keepsake box for yourself or to give as a gift.

Box Templates

heart

round

Photocopy each template, enlarging or reducing as needed to fit your box. See page 25 for transfer instructions.

Elegant Holiday Platter: Masking and Marbleizing

Dazzle your holiday guests with this simple and beautiful marbleized platter and matching serving fork. The marbleizing technique is very easy, and the ceramic paints glide smoothly onto metal and yield a lustrous finish. Create your own border motifs, such as shells and fish, flowers and leaves, or geometric shapes and spirals—your only limitation is the extent of your imagination! Then apply these simple-yet-effective techniques to create pieces you can show off all year round.

Elegant Platter Although the paints I use are designed for painting on ceramic or porcelain, they can also be used on metal, glass, or plastic. Check the labels to make sure your paints can be applied to other surfaces before you experiment. And remember not to put anything in your oven that may melt or cause toxic fumes when heated!

Step One Draw a guideline around the inner border of the platter with a china pencil, staying just along the sharp edge where the platter starts to dip down into the center. Now place transparent tape along and underneath this line. Because the line is curved, the tape will need to crimp, but it should stay smooth along the outside edge. Rub the tape down well along the drawn line.

Step Two As a starting point, mark the center of the platter rim at the top, bottom, left, and right with a china pencil. Notice that there is one holly template for the two sides and one for the top and bottom. Center the templates at these cardinal points, and tape them down. Center the snowflake templates in between the holly, and place them on the rim. Transfer the designs.

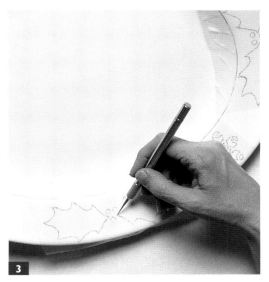

Step Three Now mask off all the transferred designs. The easiest way is to cover them with masking film (such as low-tack, easy-peel frisket), and cut along all the design lines with a utility knife. Then lift the outer film away, leaving the holly, berries, and snowflakes covered. If the film doesn't peel away easily, don't force it; it may be that you didn't cut deeply enough here or there or that you missed cutting a section entirely! Re-cut and try again. Smooth and secure the frisket well along all the edges.

Step Four Pour generous amounts of bright red and burgundy into two dishes. Mix some black in the red to make it darker. Generously load a large round brush with red, and loosely lay paint down, a section at a time, leaving some areas open. Fill those in with burgundy. Use a toothbrush to blend the two colors where they meet. Smooth out pooled areas of paint by using the brush to push the paint off the border and onto the transparent tape. (The toothbrush strokes will smooth out as the paint settles.)

51

Step Five Wait at least 24 hours after painting the border before continuing. With a utility knife, pierce the paint along the edge of the tape that masks the center of the platter. Remove the tape, pulling away from the paint. Don't force it, and remember that you can re-cut where the tape resists pulling. Using the tip of the blade, pull up the frisket on the holly, berries, and snowflakes. Don't attempt to pull the snowflake frisket up in one motion—cut it into sections, and lift it off piece by piece, re-cutting where necessary.

Step Six Clean up any paint that slipped under the frisket on the snowflakes and berries by scraping it off with the tip of your knife. Clean up the holly leaves as well, but you don't need to be too fussy here; you will be covering these areas with more paint. If you inadvertently scrape into the design, touch it up with red paint. With a moist cotton swab, clean up any paint that slipped under the tape. Air-dry and bake the platter before going on.

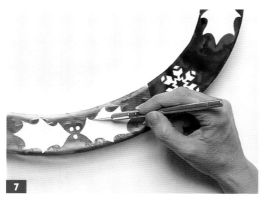

Step Seven Cover the holly again with frisket. Using a fresh knife blade, cut just outside the edge of the red, rather than directly over the line; this will ensure complete color coverage. Pull up the frisket so the holly is exposed, but leave the berries covered. Rub to secure the frisket edge.

Step Eight Using turquoise and a holiday green, paint the leaves. Blend with a toothbrush, following the procedure outlined in Step Four. Carefully lift off the frisket immediately, pulling directly up. If any paint has slipped under the film, clean it off now with a moist cotton swab.

Step Nine Paint the handle of the serving utensil with a holiday green. When it's dry, paint a squiggle down the length of the handle with the gold outliner. Then center a dot of the red outliner in each curve of the squiggle. Bake the platter and the server, and prepare to dazzle your family and guests!

Platter Templates

holly top and bottom

holly sides

snowflakes

Photocopy each template, enlarging or reducing to fit your platter and serving piece. See page 25 for transfer instructions.

Rosy Bath Ensemble:
Stylized Imagery

Brighten any bathroom with these vividly painted ceramic accessories that can be matched to any décor. The colors are interchangeable, as the stylized design is not meant to be realistic. This is another easy project for beginners. The painting technique is simple, fun, and, because it's loose and free, almost foolproof!

Innovative Style If you are decorating a bath where roses won't work, try sketching out some simple fish, shells, butterflies, or frogs. Try to keep the stylized look with just a few quick lines, or develop your own unique style, which might utilize curved or blocky lines. Have fun with it!

Step One Copy the roses template on page 57, and transfer it to the degreased piece. Each piece will require that you work out how to seam the design together to fit the shape and keep the design balanced. If you have any gaps in your transferred design, use a china pencil to draw in extra roses or leaves.

Step Two Working quickly, paint in the background with loose strokes, letting the brushstrokes show. Don't try to smooth out your strokes. If you're doing three or four pieces, by the time you've finished this step on the last piece, the paint on the first piece should be dry and ready for Step Three.

Step Three When the background is dry, paint in the leaves using the same loose brushstrokes you used in Step Two. I used two shades of green, brushing in the darker color first and blending the lighter one into it. For another attractive effect, try splitting the leaf in two, with light green on one side and dark green on the other.

Step Four You can paint the flowers with as many different colors as you like, but you might want to work out your color scheme on paper first. It's a good idea to stagger the colors for a good visual balance and so you don't have two of the same colors next to each other. If you are using four colors for seven roses, most colors will repeat once.

Step Five When all of the paint is dry to the touch, outline and detail the leaves and roses with black. Hold your brush loosely and move rather quickly as you outline each shape. If you go outside the leaf boundary a little bit into the background, it's okay; it will add movement to this free-and-easy, stylized motif.

Step Six Make sure the paint is completely dry (especially the black lines) before you continue. Clean up the top of your design with a utility knife by sliding it along the edge where the side meets the top. Scrape off the paint above the clean line (scrape lightly, or you may leave metal marks). Gently wipe off the flakes with a soft cloth or cotton pad, or blow them off. Repeat these steps for companion pieces, and let them air-dry. Bake them all, and they're ready for use.

Bath Ensemble Template

roses

Photocopy the template, enlarging or reducing as needed to fit your ceramic pieces. See page 25 for transfer instructions.

Regal Rose Teapot: Flat Washes and Painting with Metallics

A cup of Earl Grey and a scone, anyone? It's teatime, and this tea service includes a gorgeous, hand-painted rose teapot that shimmers with royal blue and glittery gold. I found this wonderful white teapot in a gourmet coffee shop and happily scooped it up because of its unusual shape. The design I demonstrate here, however, can be applied to any shape. Shop around for your own special teapot!

Royal Teapot This elegant teapot will be right at home at a formal tea. It's painted with flat washes, trimmed in glittering gold metallic paint, and decorated with a beautiful rose.

1

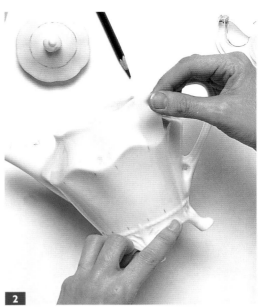

2

Step One Your teapot will probably be a different shape than mine. If it is as ornate as mine is, try to design your color breaks according to the natural shape of the teapot surface. Otherwise, for more commonly and simply shaped teapots, you can try the suggestions drawn above for your design treatments.

Step Two On the teapot, use transparent tape to mask off the areas between the panels you plan to paint. On the lid, draw a circle with a china pencil about halfway down the lid. You can mask off the top if you want, but I would have had to crimp the tape too much for my lid, so I used a drawn line as a guide.

3

Step Three Apply the color one panel at a time. If your panels are close together, make sure the tape between them is cut down the middle for easy removal. Using a wide, flat brush loaded well with blue, brush in one direction with light strokes until you have covered the panel evenly. Watch for pools of paint that may form into drips as the paint dries. Remove the tape immediately. Prop up the pot while it dries, keeping the panels as level as possible.

Step Four Paint a wash on the lid in the same manner as you did the pot, moving around the lid and stroking down and off the edge as you go. If you masked this area first, be sure to remove the tape immediately after painting.

Step Five Create a clean line at the ridge of the pot by sliding a utility blade—held at a stable angle—across the ridge, scraping off the paint. Clean up the rest of the paint edges on both pieces with a knife or a moist cotton swab. Wait the designated air-drying time, and bake both the pot and the lid.

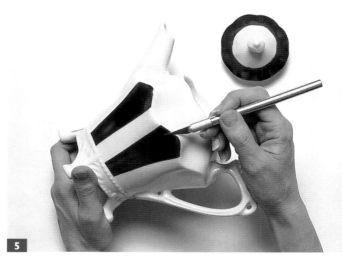

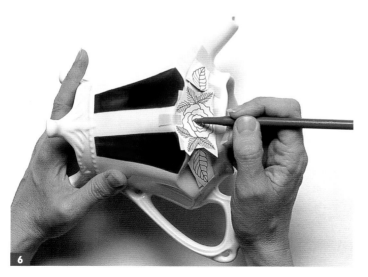

Step Six Transfer the rose design onto the pot. You may have to cut it apart or add a leaf to fit your designated area—whatever works with your teapot. This step requires a lot of handling, so you'll be glad you've baked the piece first! Just be careful not to leave fingerprints on any areas still to be painted. If you're concerned about handling the piece, you might want to wear gloves while painting the rest of the pot.

Step Seven Paint the ferns with a soft turquoise color. I used a liner brush to get even, thin lines, but a round brush will work too. Keep your strokes light, and paint the stem line first. Paint the leaves by starting at the stem with a swift outward stroke, quickly lifting the brush as you complete the stroke to make a sharp, tapered point at the end.

Step Eight Paint the rose one petal at a time, taking care not to touch any wet paint. Begin with a stripe of red along the outside petal edge. Then paint fuchsia in the middle and burgundy along the inside edge. Blend by jiggling your brush back and forth. Highlight the inner petals with a thin stroke of white along their outer edges.

Step Nine Choose a dark green for the leaves, and create a lighter green by mixing this color with white. Load a 1/4" flat brush with two colors: Dip one side of the brush in light green and the other side in dark green, as shown on the top brush. Paint the leaf sections in halves by making S strokes that end at the middle of the leaf. Make the S strokes smaller as you work toward the tip of the leaf. Then repeat this process on the other leaf half. Load your brush as often as you need to, wiping it between loads so that the paint doesn't blend so much that you lose the variegated look.

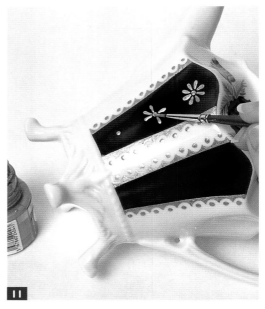

Step Ten Transfer the border design to the edges of the stripes. Working on one side of the stripe at a time, mask off the edge of the stripe with transparent tape. Then paint the border with metallic gold. Pull off the tape, and clean up the edges of the border with a utility knife, making the points sharp and neat. Sketch the scallops onto the lid with a china pencil, and then paint the gold on the lid.

Step Eleven Paint three dots inside each blue stripe on the teapot, centering them and leaving enough room around them for adding petals. Using a small round brush and the one-stroke painting method (page 8), start by painting petals at the four cardinal points. Then paint the petals in between, making eight petals total for each flower. Always paint toward the middle and lift off gradually.

Step Twelve Now paint the gold trim. I followed the design sculpted into my teapot for the legs at the base, and decided not to cover the entire handle, since there is only a small amount of gold on the spout. Remember: You can always remove what you don't like with a moist cotton swab. Bake the pieces, and you're ready for high tea!

Teapot Templates

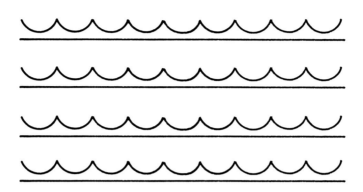

borders

rose option 1

rose option 2

Photocopy each template, enlarging or reducing as needed to fit your teapot. See page 25 for transfer instructions.

A World of Possibilities

After you've explored the different techniques in this book, you'll want to combine them in your own unique ways. Creating stunning works of art that are both useful and gift-worthy is a fully satisfying experience. These wonderful bake-at-home paints have made ceramic painting a breeze, and you're sure to find a vast array of ceramic, china, and porcelain pieces to inspire your creativity.

I recommend that you keep a notebook or journal where you can scribble, sketch, or paste ideas or inspirations you come across. After you begin painting ceramics, you'll develop an eye for the right pieces. When you see an interesting piece, make a note of where you saw it. You may even find a beautiful fabric pattern or a great color combination that you want to remember for future reference. As you keep track of these ideas, more inspiration will come to you. Then all you have to do is turn your ideas into colorful reality!

Express Yourself There is no standard to meet or color schemes to comply with; it's all a matter of your own individual style and taste. So plunge ahead boldly, and revel in the endless possibilities of ceramic painting!